PIANO • VOCAL • GUITAR

the JAMAICAN MUSIC SONGBOOK

REGGAE & BEYOND

T005113S

ISBN 0-7935-9322-0

HAL•LEONARD® CORPORATION

7777 W. BLUEMOUND RD. P.O. BOX 13819 MILWAUKEE, WI 53213

Visit Hal Leonard Online at
www.halleonard.com

CONTENTS

BREDDA GRAVALICIOUS

By WINSTON MATTHEWS

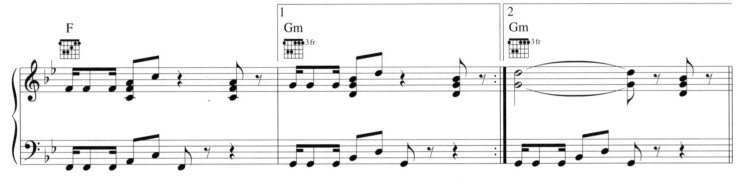

Bred-da Grav-a-li-cious, I say you're too damn ___

care - ful. Bred-da Grav-a-li-cious, I say you're

D.S. al Coda

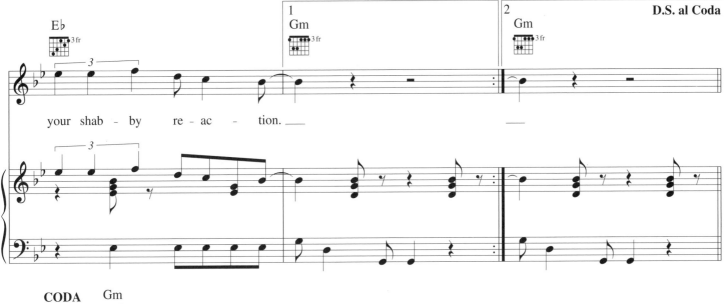

your shab – by re – ac – tion. ___

CODA

I   sit   in   the

sum – mer   schools   and   the   greed – y   doth   lose   his   gold ___   to   the   re –

CARRY GO BRING COME

By JUSTIN HINES

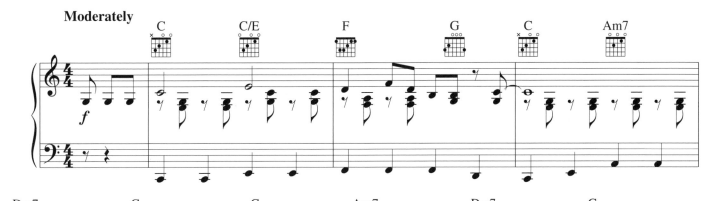

Please   car - ry   go   bring __ come   my dear; __
com - ing from home __   to   go; __
meek shall in - her - it   the   earth, __
4., 5. *(See additional lyrics)*

__   bring   me   drink. __
__   make   sure   'bout   this. __
__   you old   Jez - e - bel. __

Please
It's

Additional Lyrics

4. It's better to sleep at home, you won't die outside,
   Instead of keeping your dread thoughts on one-a innocent one.

5. For time will tell on you, you old Jezebel.
   How long shall the weakened reign over my people?

CHERRY OH BABY

Words and Music by
ERIC DONALDSON

Moderately Fast

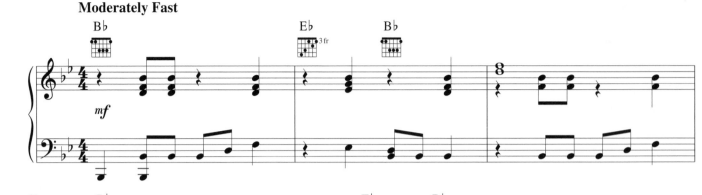

Oh, cher - ry oh, cher - ry oh, ba - by,
Oh, cher - ry oh, cher ry oh, ba - by,

don't you know I'm in need __ of thee? If you don't be -
can't you see I'm in love __ with you? If you don't be -

COUNTRY BOY

By LEROY SIBBLES

CURLY LOCKS

By LEE PERRY

two roads be - fore you; which one will be your

choice? ____ I real - ly wan - na know now.

Repeat and Fade | **Optional Ending**

EVERYTHING I OWN

Words and Music by
DAVID GATES

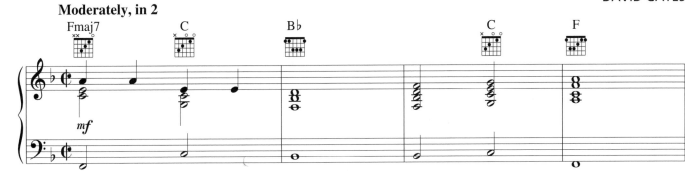

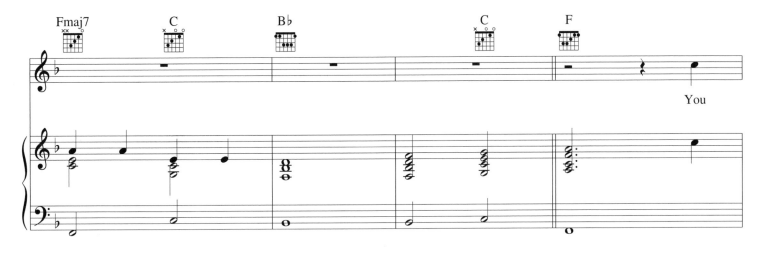

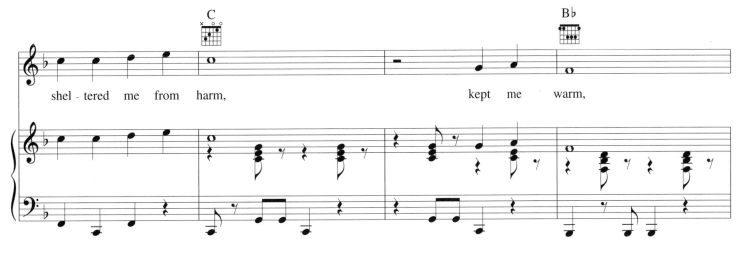

You gave my life to me,

set me free, set me

free. The fin - est years

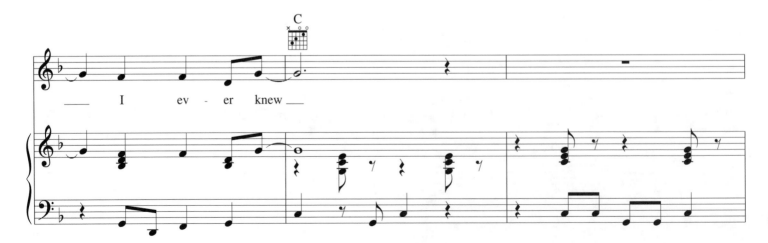

I ev - er knew

is all ___ the years ___ I had with you. And

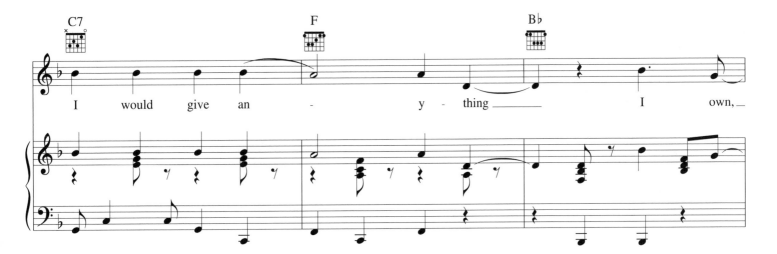

I would give an - y thing ___ I own, ___

give up my life, ___ my heart, ___

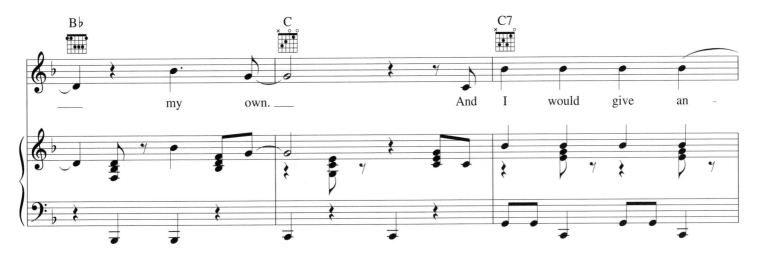

___ my own. ___ And I would give an -

-y - thing _____ I own _____ just to

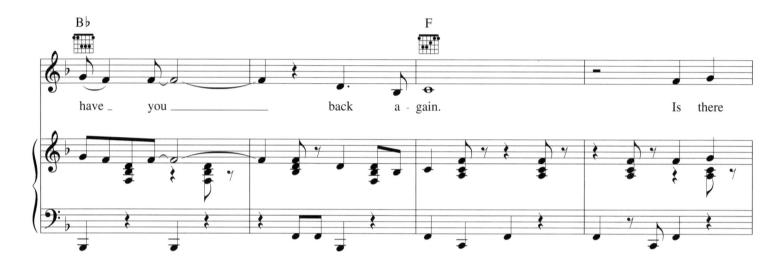

have _ you _____ back a - gain. Is there

some - one you know _____ that won't let you go _____ and

tak - ing it all _____ for grant - ed? You may

lose them one day; _____ some - one takes them a - way _____ and you

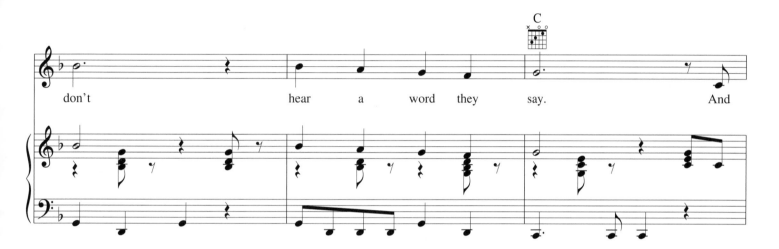

don't hear a word they say. And

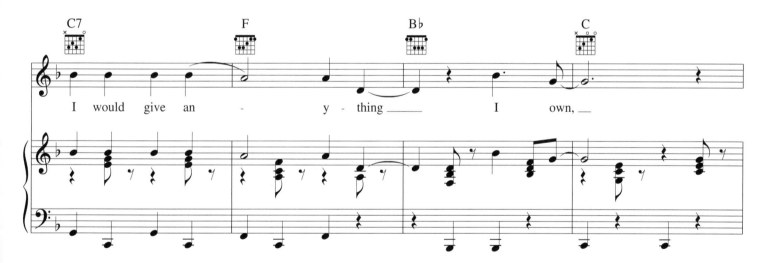

I would give an - y - thing _____ I own, _____

give up my life, _____ my heart _____ my own. _____ And

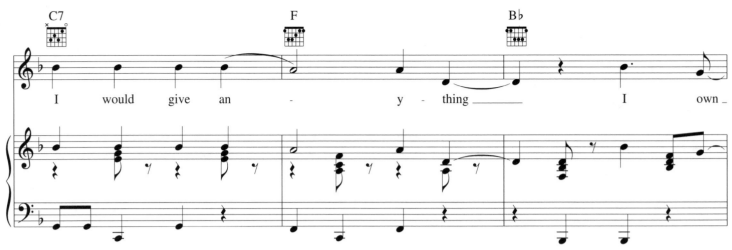

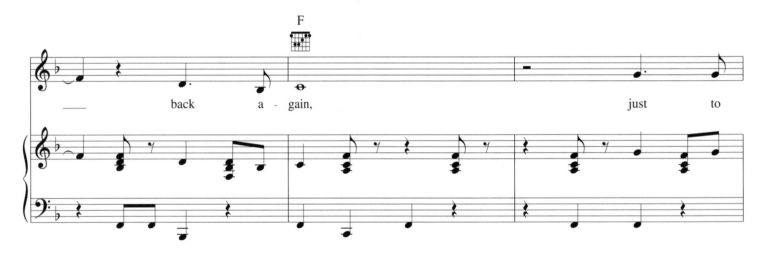

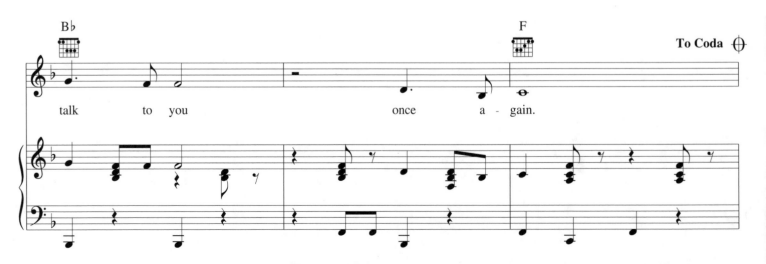

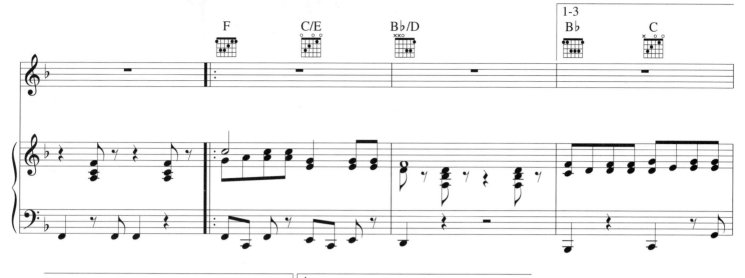

D.S. al Coda

If there's

CODA

Just to hold ____ you ____ once a-

talk ____ to you once a-

Repeat and Fade

gain.

Optional Ending

Just to gain.

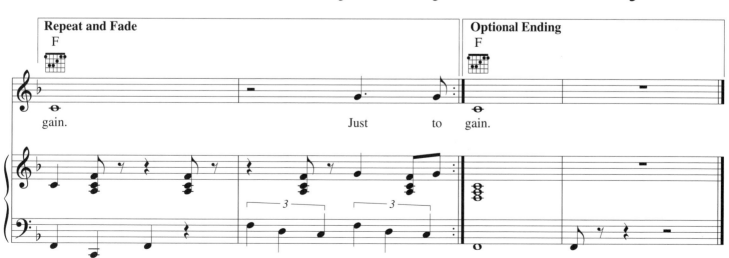

THE HARDER THEY COME

By JIMMY CLIFF

waiting for me when I die. ___
tryin' to drive me un-der-ground. ___
though I know that when you're dead you can't.

But be-tween ___ the day ___ you're born ___ and a-when you die, ___
And they think ___ that they ___ have got ___ the bat-tle won ___
But I'd rath-er be ___ a free ___ man in my grave, ___

___ they nev-er seem to hear ___
___ I say for-give ___ them, Lord, they know ___
___ than liv-ing as a pup-

HOUSEWIFE'S CHOICE

By DERRICK MORGAN

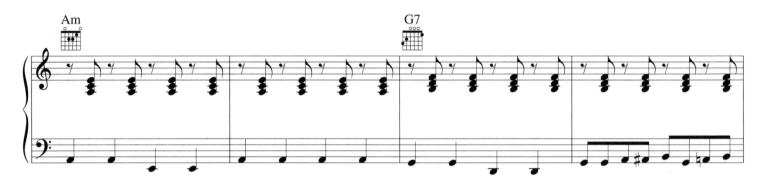

should know I _____ love you. _____ 'Cause _____ my

heart, dear, is trem-bling like _____ a leaf.

Sax solo ad. lib

I'M STILL WAITING

Words and Music by
BOB MARLEY

Ev - 'ry lit - tle beat my heart beats, girl, _____ it's
You know, you know I love you. That's

at your door. I just wan - na love you
why _____ I wait my whole life through.

and I'm nev - er gon - na hurt _____ you, girl.
My _____ part - ing to you

So, won't you come out to me now, _____ girl?
for be - ing what _ I _____ am.

THE ISRAELITES

Words and Music by
DESMOND DEKKER

Moderately

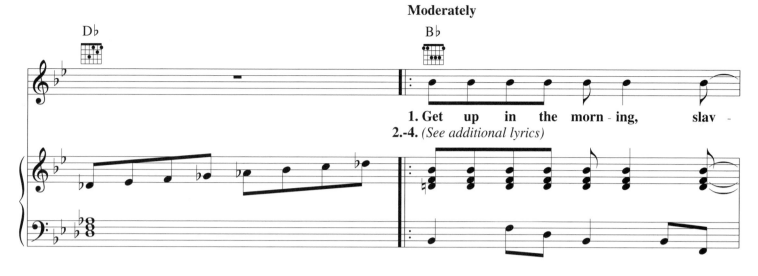

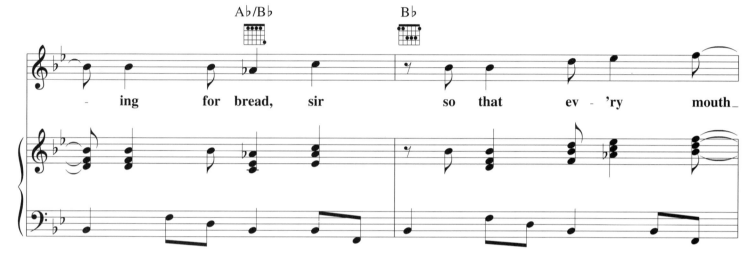

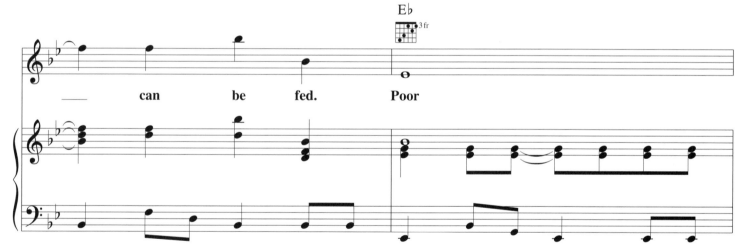

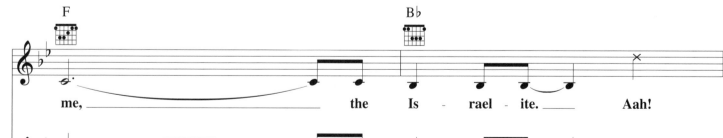

Additional Lyrics

2. My wife and my kids, they pack up and leave me;
"Darling," she said, "I'm yours to receive."
Poor me, the Israelite. Aah!

3. Shirt them ah tear up, trousers are gone;
I don't want to end up like Bonnie and Clyde.
Poor me, the Israelite. Aah!

4. After a storm there must be a calm,
They catch me in the farm, you sound the alarm.
Poor me, the Israelite. Aah!

MISS JAMAICA

By JIMMY CLIFF

Moderate Shuffle

lyrics:

Ro - ses are red, __ vio - lets are blue, __ be - lieve me, __ I love you. __ Let's not be a - part __ 'cause you're the rose of my heart, __ and sweet rose, you are my queen.

Miss __ Ja - mai - ca, ____ Miss __ Ja - mai - ca. ____

Repeat and Fade

Optional Ending

MARCUS GARVEY

By WINSTON RODNEY
and PHILLIP FULLWOOD

Mar - cus Gar - vey words come to pass. __

Mar - cus Gar - vey words come to pass. __

Can't get __ no food __ to eat. __

Can't get no mon-ey to spend. _____

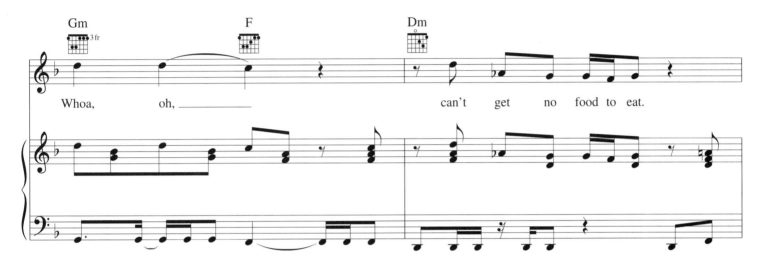

Gm   F   Dm

Whoa, oh, _____   can't get no food to eat.

Gm   F   Dm

Mm, _____   can't get no mon-ey to spend.

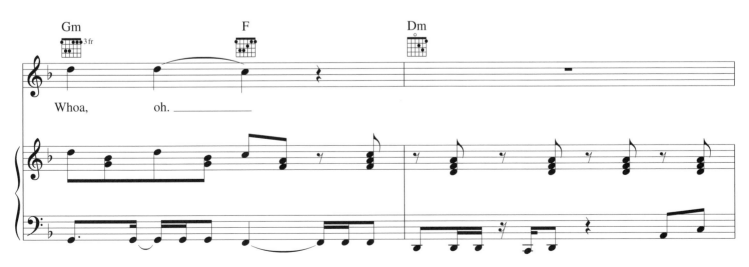

Gm   F   Dm

Whoa, oh. _____

Calm lead - er want no let me do what I can, for

you, and you, and you, hel -

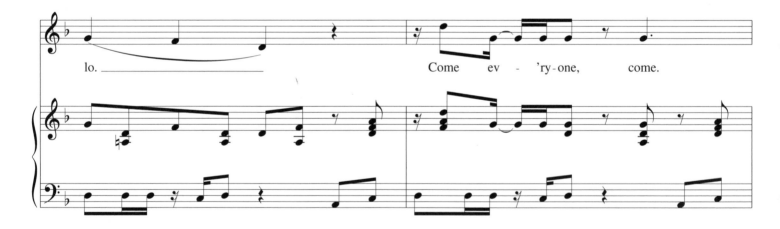

lo. Come ev - 'ry-one, come.

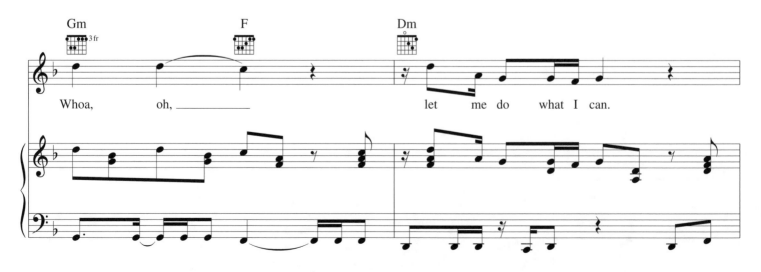

Whoa, oh, let me do what I can.

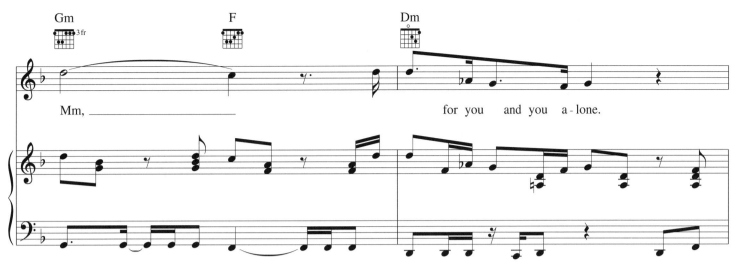

Mm, _____ for you and you a-lone.

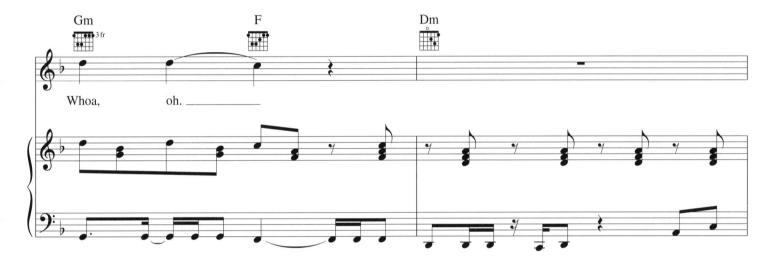

Whoa, oh. _____

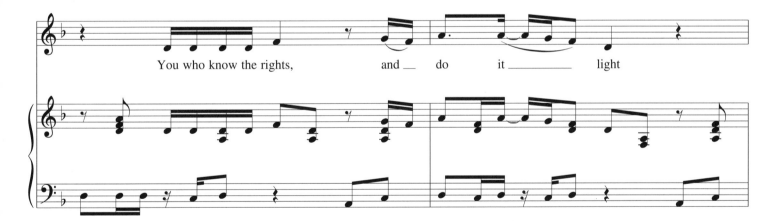

You who know the rights, and __ do it _____ light

shall be spanked __ with man-y stripes. __

Been, ___ been un-will - ing, I'm warn - ing ___

You ___ got your-self ___ to blame. I tell you,

do right, _ do right, do right, do right, do right ___

Do right, _ do right, do right, do right, do right, _ do right, ___ I beg you.

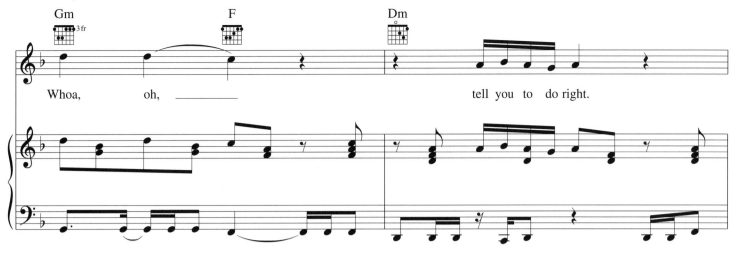

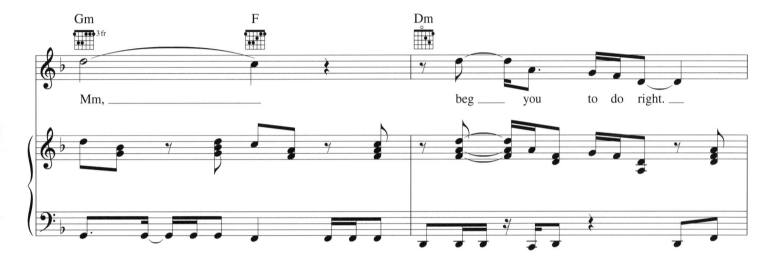

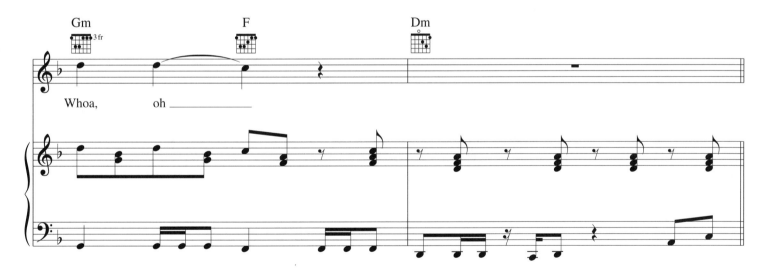

Where is Pa-co_ Well?_ He's

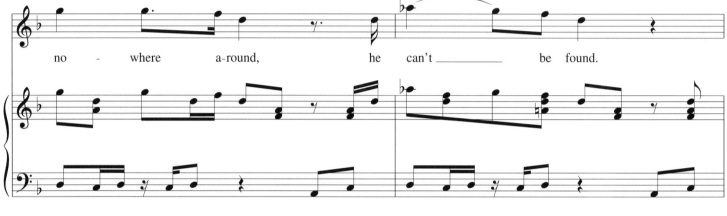

no - where a-round, he can't _____ be found.

First _____ be-tray - er, _____ who gave a-way Mar - cus

Gar - vey. That's what I'm say-in', Tahn.

First _____ prize, _ catch _ them, Gar - vey. _ Whoa, oh, _____

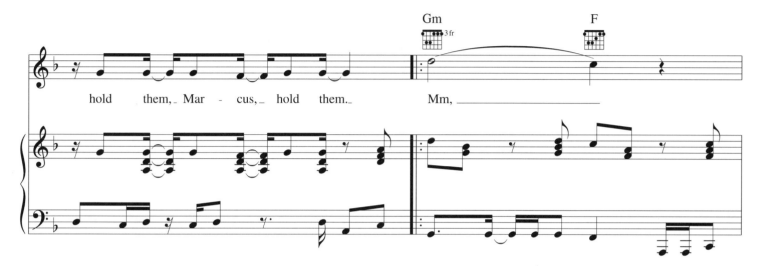

hold them, _ Mar - cus, _ hold them. Mm, _____

proph - e - cy of _ whole fear. _ Whoa, oh, _____ catch them, _ Gar - vey, _ catch them. _

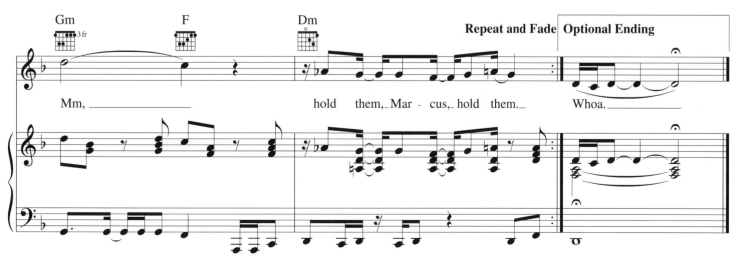

Mm, _____ hold them, _ Mar - cus, _ hold them. _ Whoa. _____

MURDER SHE WROTE

By SLY DUNBAR, LLOYD WILLIS,
EVERTON BONNER and JOHN TAYLOR

Mur - der, she _____ wrote. _____ Mur - der, she wrote. _

Mur - der, she _____ wrote. _

Play 4 times

Rap: see Rap lyrics

Have a co - zy con a - when she
love with a cool Chi - nese, white

Rap Lyrics

I'll kill all of them.
A pretty fearsome bunch come around town.
Then they kind of live in town,
All chopped up. Follow me.
A pretty fearsome bunch come around town.
Then they kind of live in town,
All discussin' that you're pretty,
They - a said, pretty bunch of character.
Dirty that you is - a up to.
Flirty, flirty, you are the town pick
And are so - orry a - when you find your mischief.
You tell them you're sorry, sorry, sorry.

NO WOMAN NO CRY

Words and Music by
VINCENT FORD

said I re-mem-ber when we used to sit

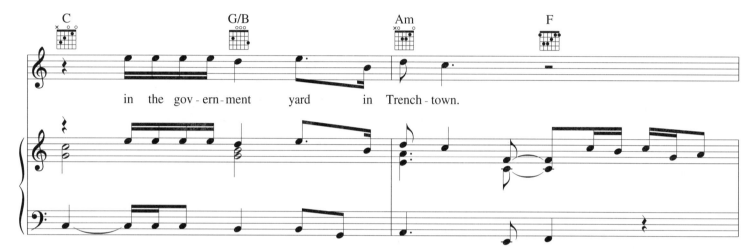

in the gov-ern-ment yard in Trench-town.

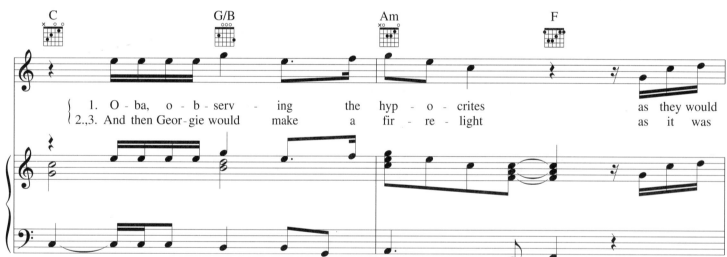

1. O-ba, o-b-serv-ing the hyp-o-crites   as they would
2.,3. And then Geor-gie would make a fir-re-light   as it was

min-gle with the good peo-ple we meet,
log wood burn-in' through the night.

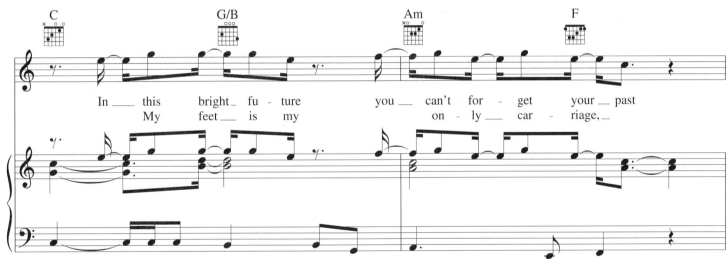

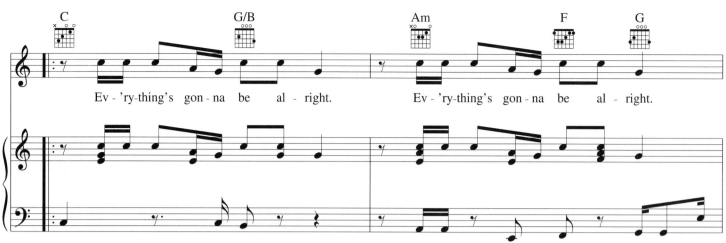

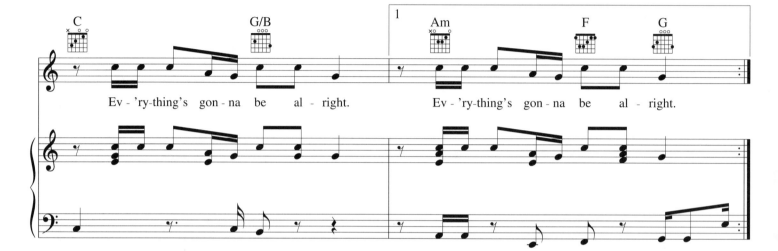

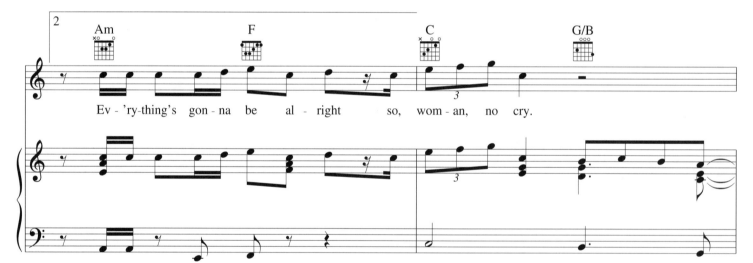

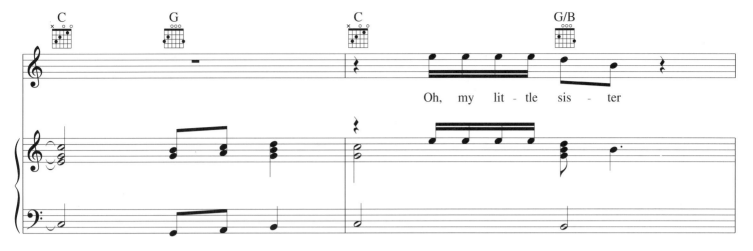

Oh, my lit - tle sis - ter

don't shed no tears. ___ No wom - an, no cry.

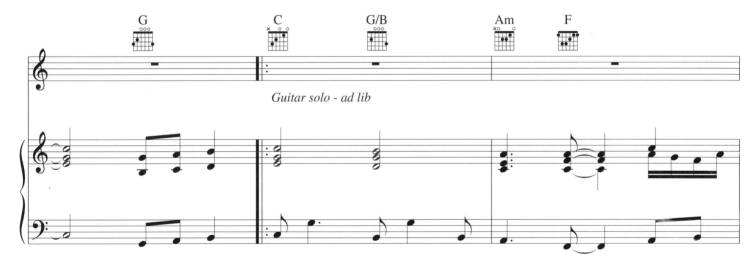

Guitar solo - ad lib

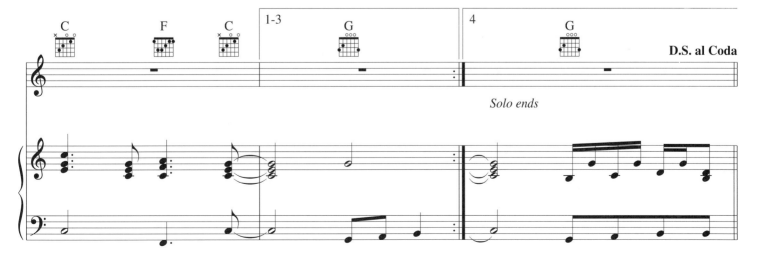

Solo ends

D.S. al Coda

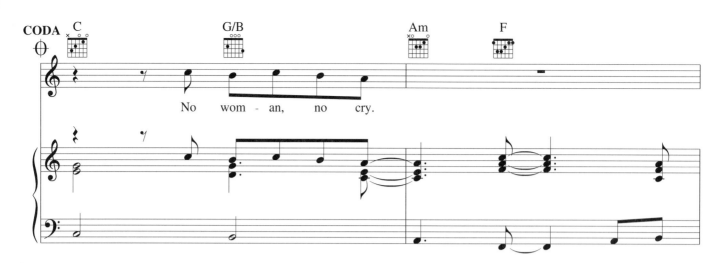

No wom - an, no cry.

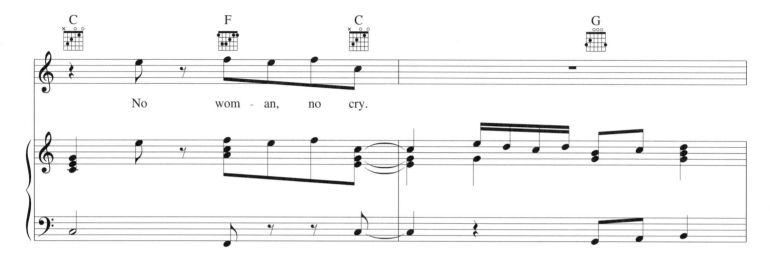

No wom - an, no cry.

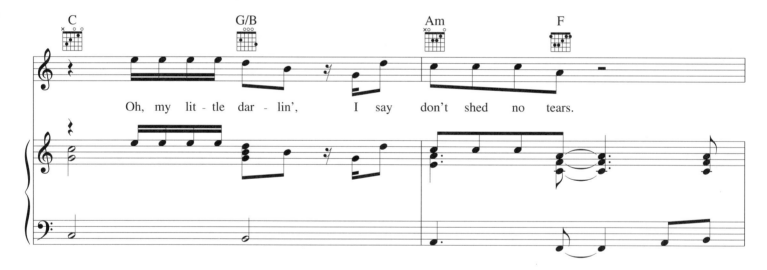

Oh, my lit - tle dar - lin', I say don't shed no tears.

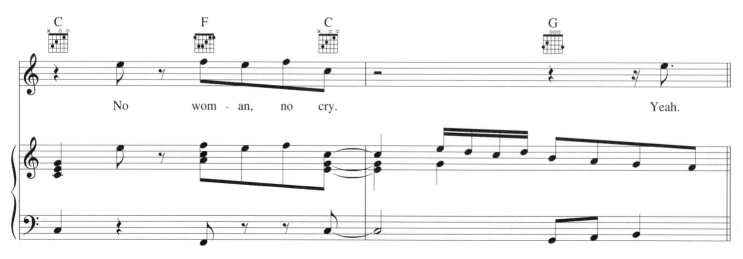

No wom - an, no cry.   Yeah.

Lit - tle dar - lin', don't shed no tears. ___
Vocal tacet 3rd time

No wom - an, no cry.

Play 3 times

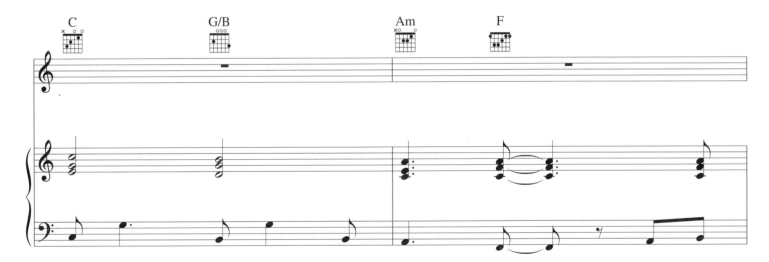

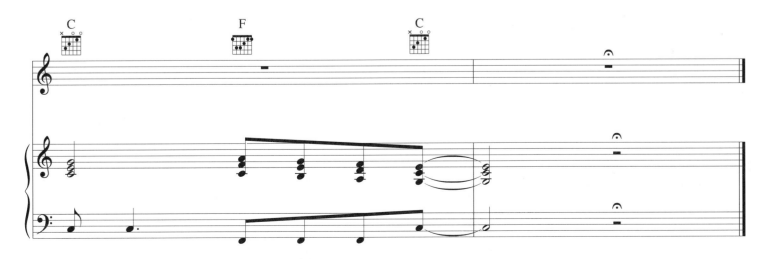

POLICE AND THIEVES

By JUNIOR MURVIN
and LEE PERRY

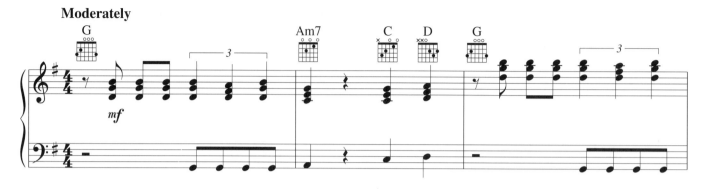

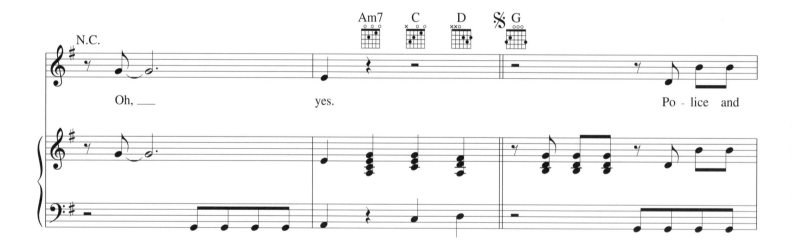

Oh, ___ yes. Po - lice and

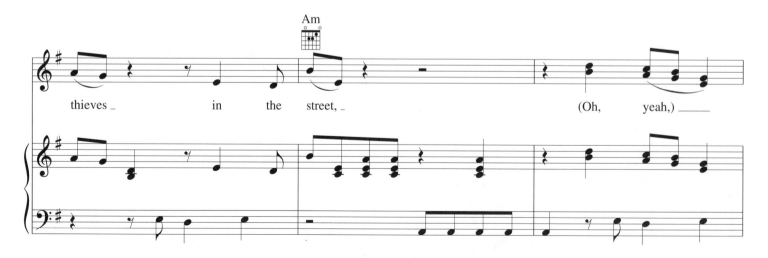

thieves ___ in the street, ___ (Oh, yeah,) ___

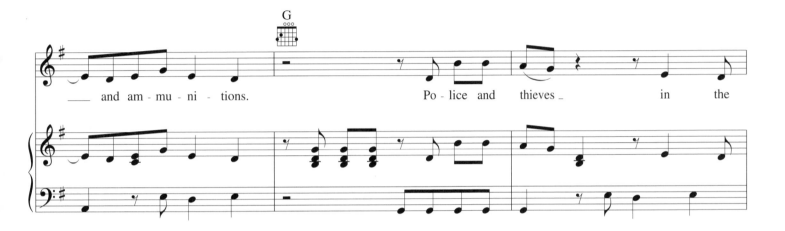

Plung-ing their sin _____ to rev-a-

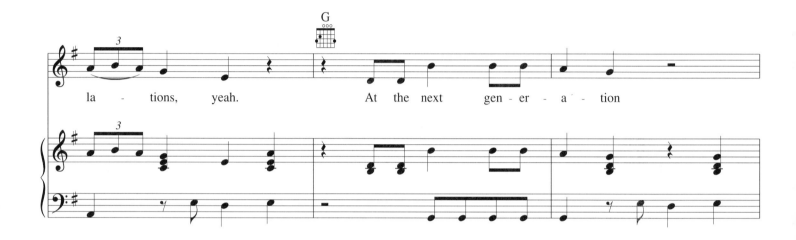

la - tions, yeah. At the next gen-er-a-tion

we'll be, hear me. All the

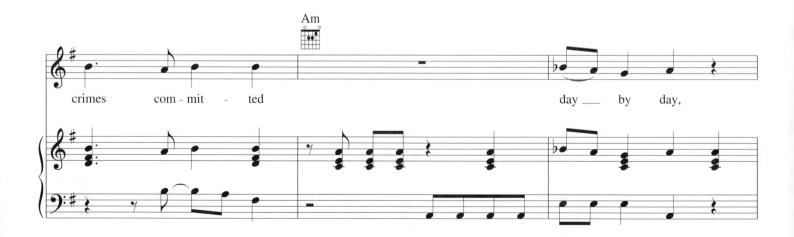

crimes com-mit-ted day _____ by day,

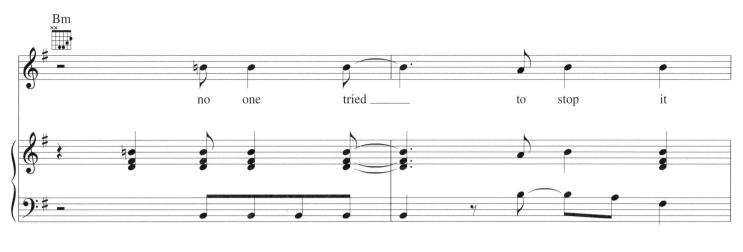

D.S. al Coda

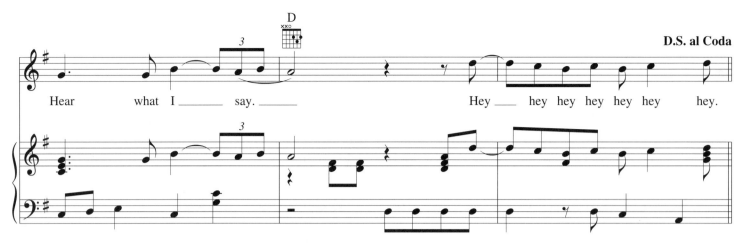

Hear   what I _____ say. _____   Hey ___ hey hey hey hey hey   hey.

CODA

Mm doot mm day   doot mm day   doot

dot mm dot ___ mm day   dah.   Mm doot mm

day   doot mm day   doot mm dot mm dot ___ mm day   dah. (Oh,   yeah.) ____

Mm doot mm day doot mm day doot mm dot mm dot ___ mm day

dah. Mm doot doo dway dot doo doo dway dot doo doo dway dot doo doo dot mm dot ___

___ mm dot ___ mm dah dot, mm. ___ All the

crimes com-mit-ted day ___ by day,

no one tried ___ to stop it

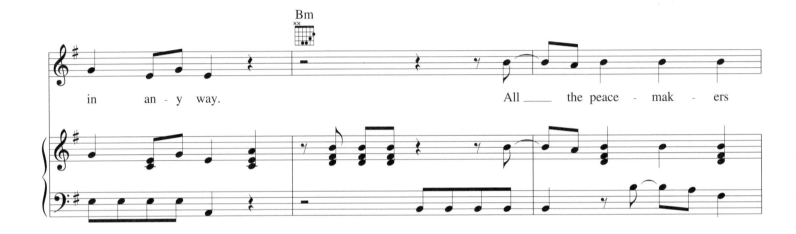

in an - y way.   All ___ the peace - mak - ers

turn ___ war of - fi - cers.

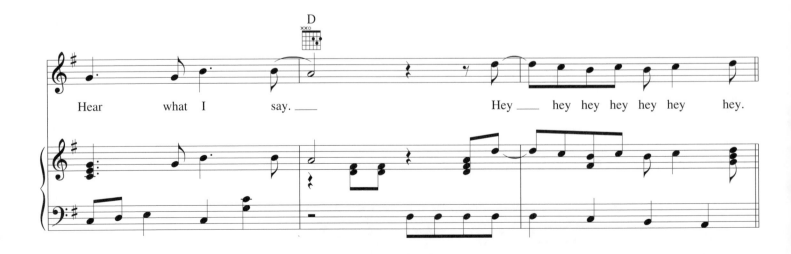

Hear   what   I   say. ___   Hey ___ hey hey hey hey hey   hey.

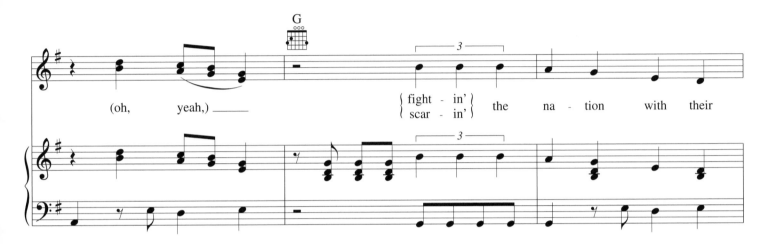

RIVER JORDAN

By LINCOLN MINOTT

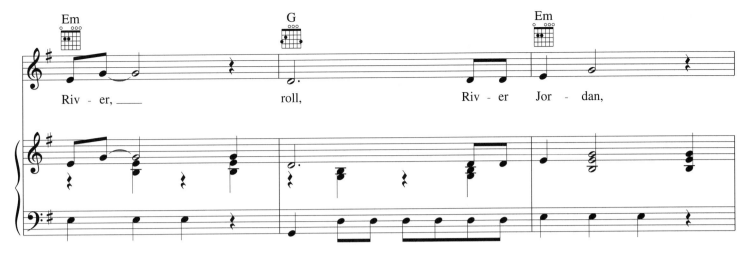

Riv - er, ___ roll, Riv - er Jor - dan,

call - ing us home, ___ call - ing us home. ___

___ We got to go back home, ___

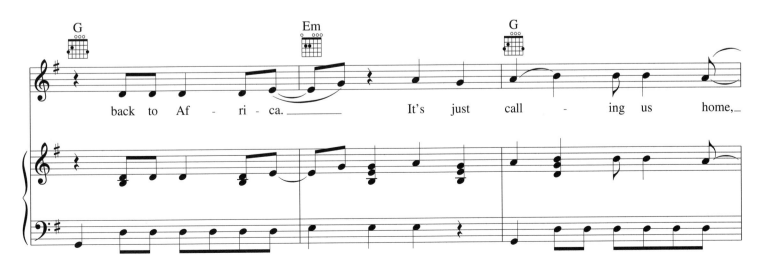

back to Af - ri - ca. ___ It's just call - ing us home, ___

been down _____ in slav - 'ry, _____ well, _____

and __ now _____ we just got to be free. _____

D.S. al Coda

Yes, we want to be free, _____ well. _____

CODA Em

So long we've been bound _____ in

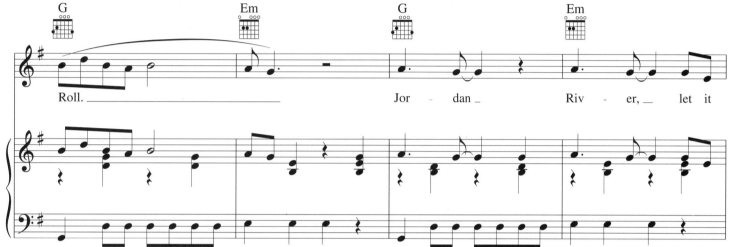

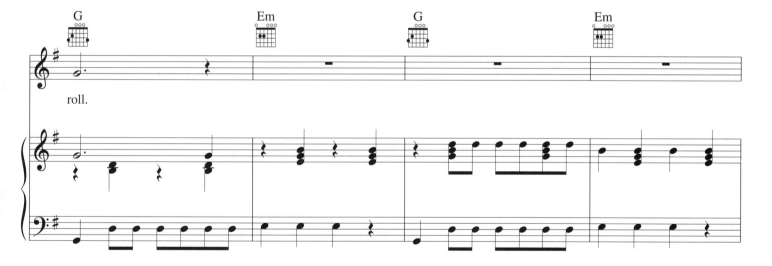

and ___ now _____ we just

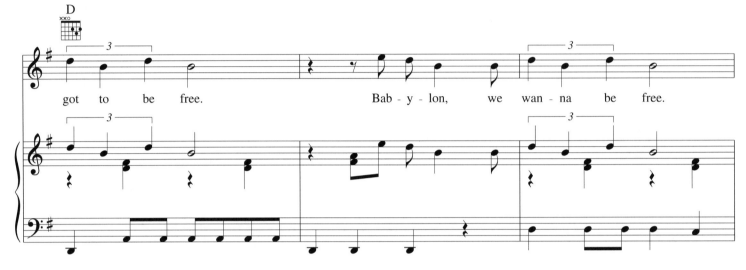

got to be free. Bab - y - lon, we wan - na be free.

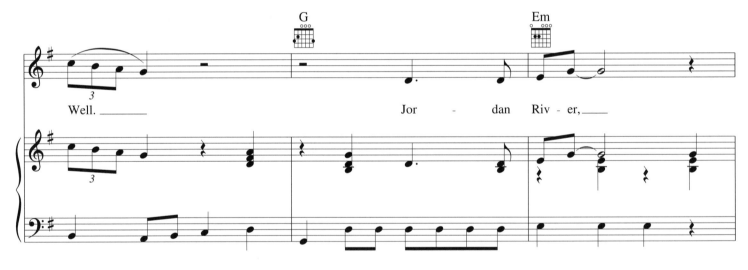

Well. _____ Jor - dan Riv - er, _____

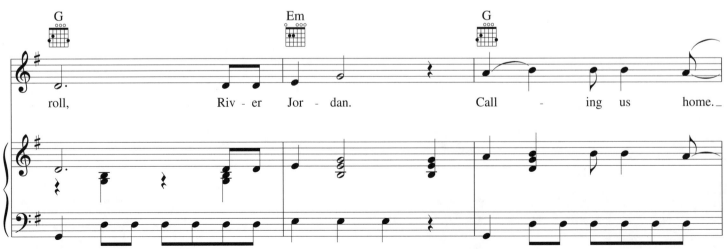

roll, Riv - er Jor - dan. Call - ing us home. _

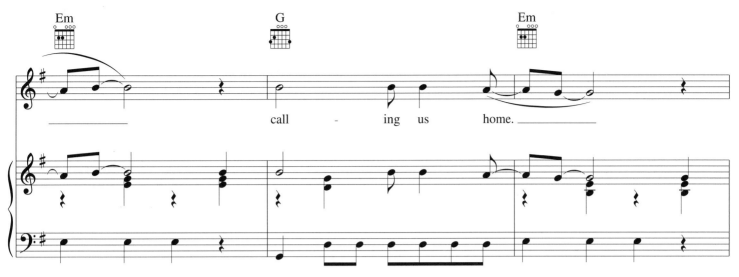

call - ing us home.

we got to bo gack home, _____ back to Af - ri - ca. _____

_____ It's just call - ing us home, _____ call - ing us home, _____

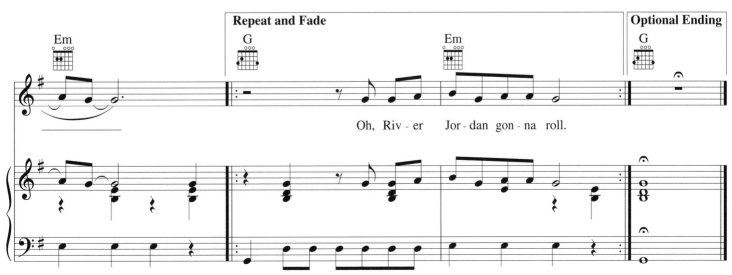

Repeat and Fade **Optional Ending**

Oh, Riv - er Jor - dan gon - na roll.

RIVERS OF BABYLON

Words and Music by BRENT DOWE,
JAMES A. McNAUGHTON, GEORGE REYAM
and FRANK FARIAN

Zi - on. ___ 'Cause the wick - ed ___ car - ried us a - way, cap -

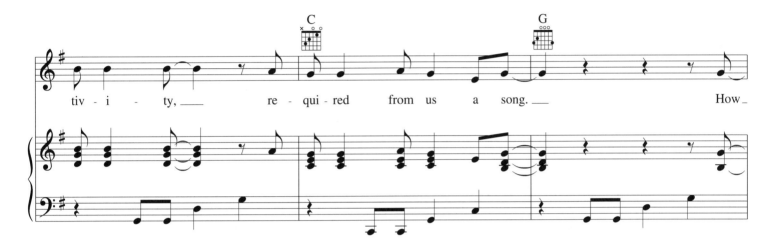

tiv - i - ty, ___ re - qui - red from us a song. ___ How ___

___ can we sing King of ___ our song in a strange ___ land? ___

'Cause the wick - ed ___ car - ried us a - way, cap -

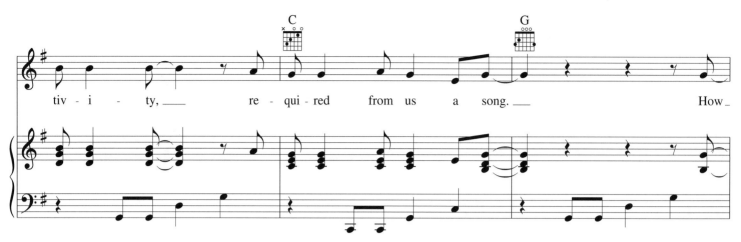

tiv-i-ty, ___ re-qui-red from us a song. ___ How_

___ can we sing King of ___ our song ___ in a strange _____ land?

___ Sing it out loud. ___ (Ah. _____) Sing a song of free-dom, { broth-er. / sis-ter. }

(Ah. _____) Sing a song of free-dom, { bro - broth-er. ___ / sis - sis-ter. ___ }

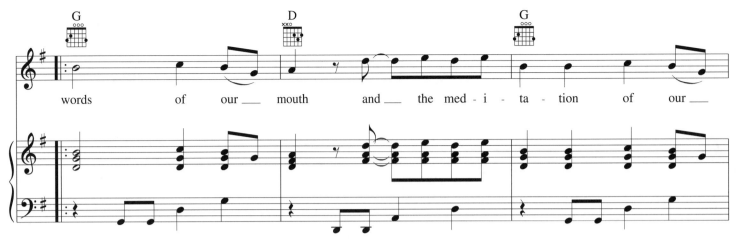

words of our ___ mouth and ___ the med-i-ta-tion of our ___

heart be ac-cept-a-ble in Thy ___ sight, oh for right. ___

So let the right. ___ Sing it out loud. ___ (Ah. ___

___) We got to sing ___ it to-geth-er. (Ah. ___) Ev-'ry one of us. ___

(Ah ah ah ah.) La la la la la _____ la la. (Ah ah ah

ah.) Whoa ___ whoa _____ whoa. ___ (Ah. _____)

(Ah. _____)

D.S. and Fade | **Optional Ending**

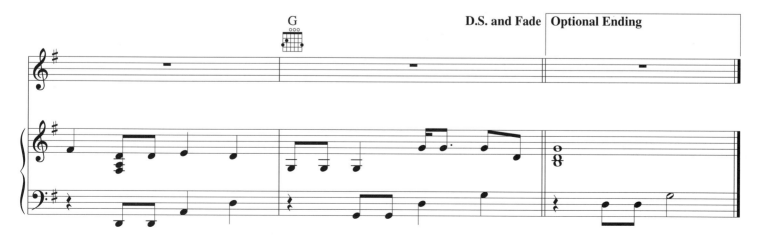

SIMMER DOWN

By BOB MARLEY

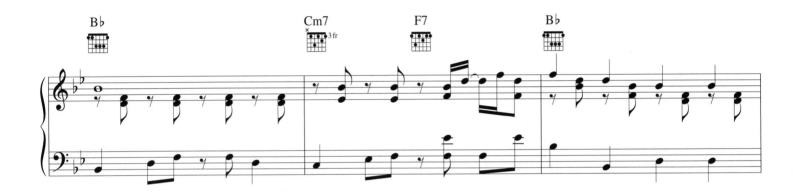

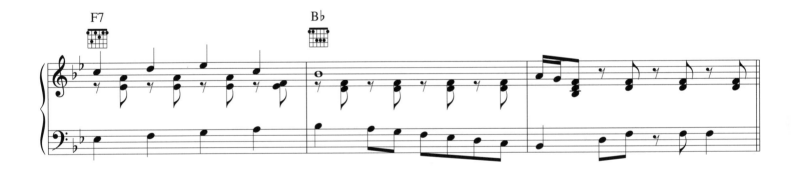

Sim-mer down. _____ You're look-ing too hot, so sim-mer down.

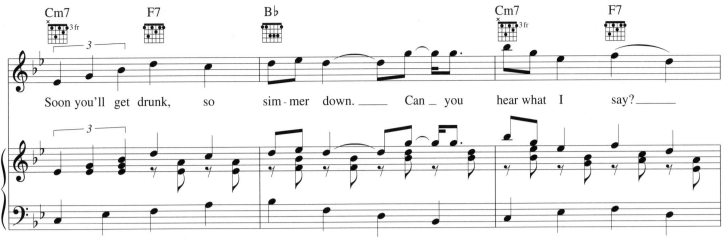

Soon you'll get drunk, so sim-mer down.___ Can_ you hear what I say?___

Sim-mer down._____ Then why won't you, why won't you, why won't you sim-mer down?

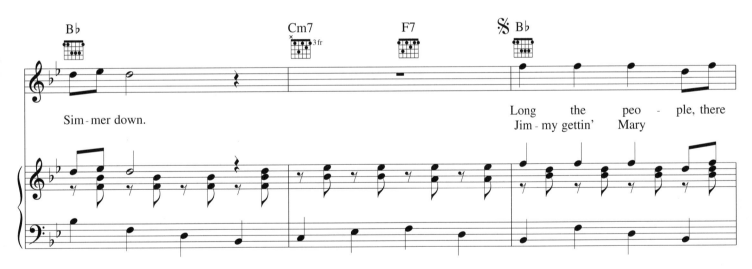

Sim-mer down.

Long the peo-ple, there
Jim-my gettin' Mary

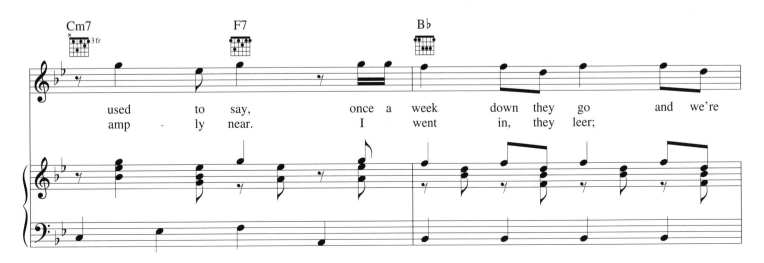

used to say, once a week down they go and we're
amp-ly near. I went in, they leer;

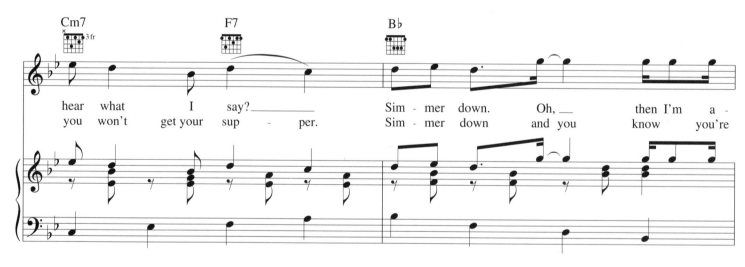

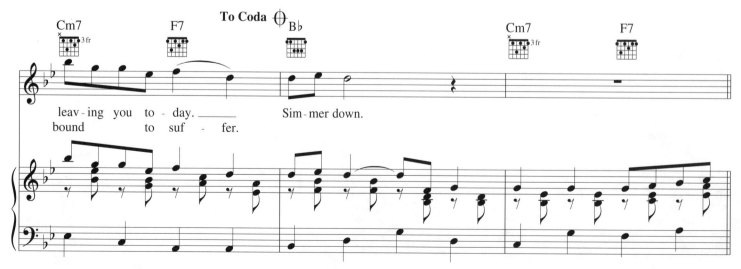

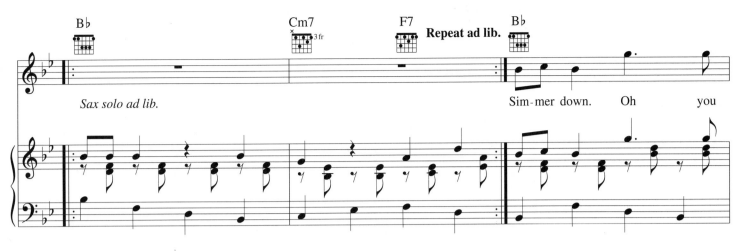

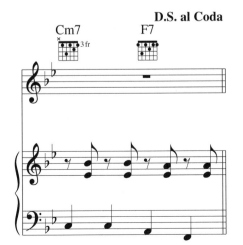

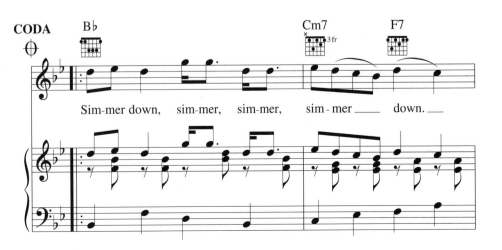

SIX AND SEVEN BOOKS

By FREDERICK HIBBERT

Bright two-beat

Ooh, _____ the six and the

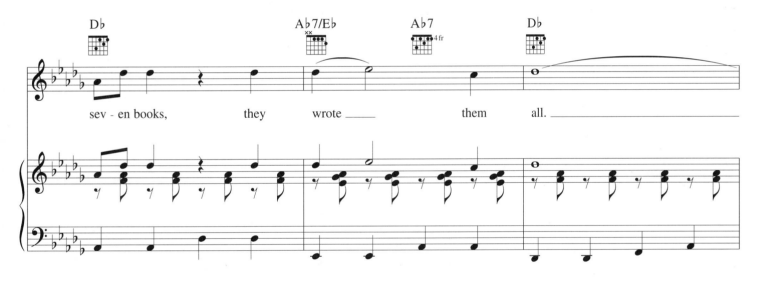

sev - en books, they wrote _____ them all. _____

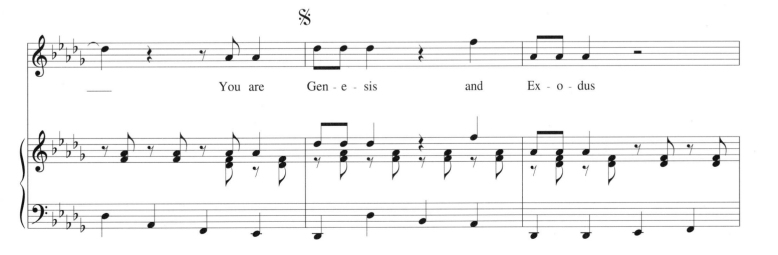

_____ You are Gen - e - sis and Ex - o - dus

Le-vit-i-cus and __ Num - bers, Deu-ter-on-o-my and

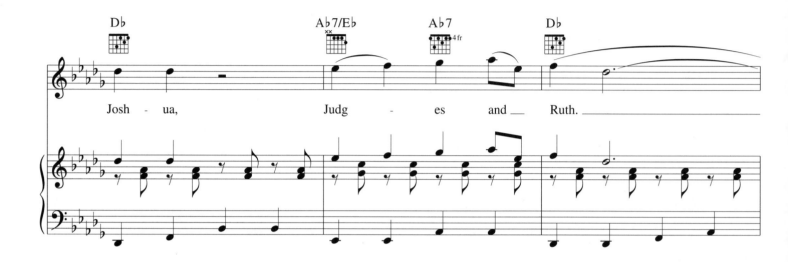

Josh - ua, Judg - es and __ Ruth. _____

__ Oh, the six and the sev-en books, they

wrote _____ them all. Oh, the

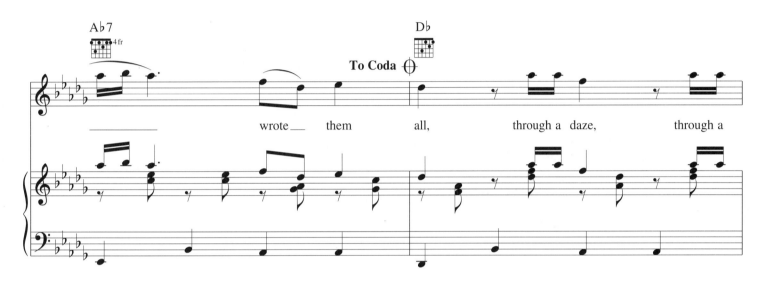

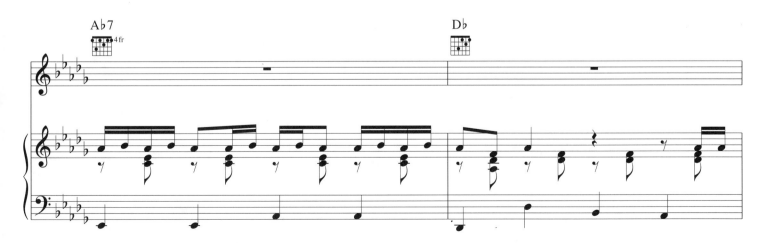

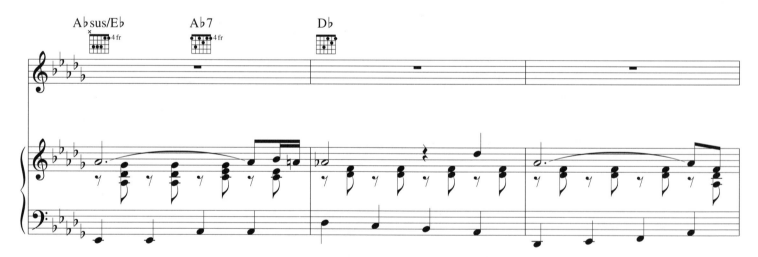

Whoa. _ You are

all. Oh, the six and the sev - en books, they _____

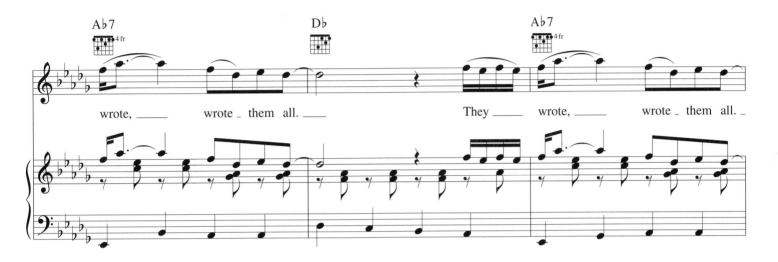

wrote, _____ wrote ___ them all. _____ They _____ wrote, _____ wrote ___ them all. _

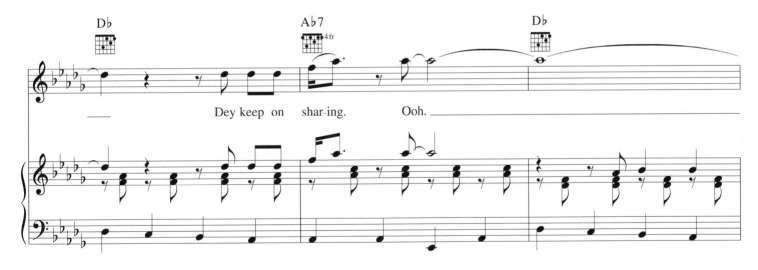

___ Dey keep on shar - ing. Ooh. _____

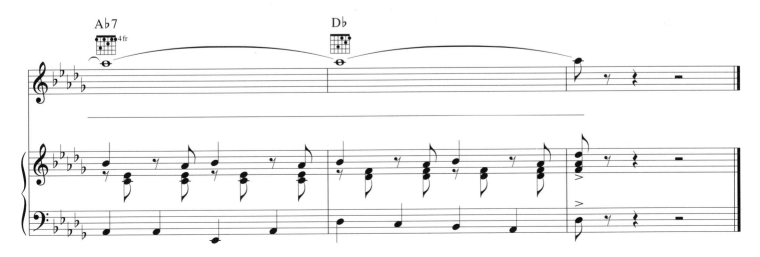

TOUGHER THAN TOUGH

By DERRICK MORGAN

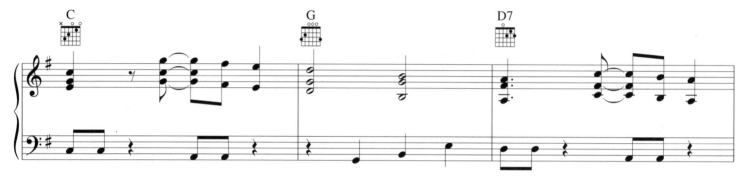

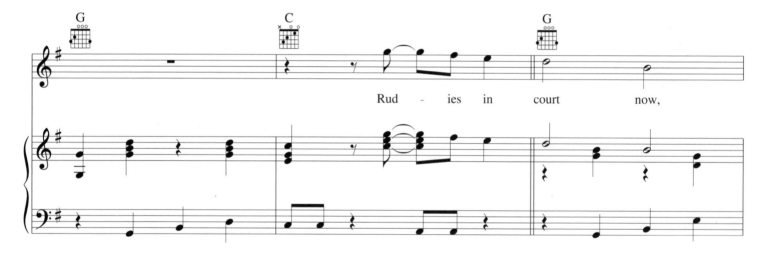

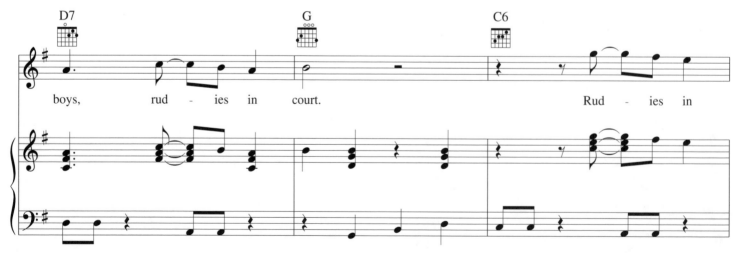

Rud - ies in court now,

boys, rud - ies in court. Rud - ies in

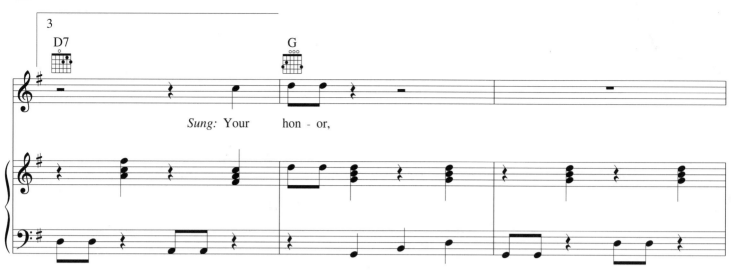

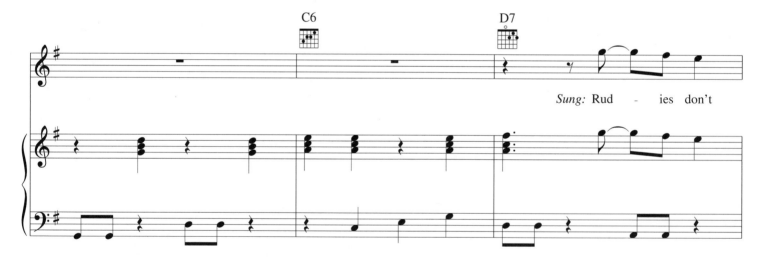

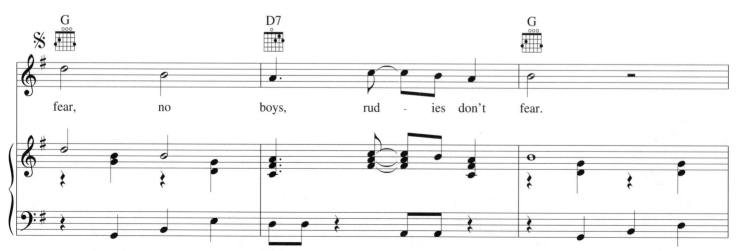

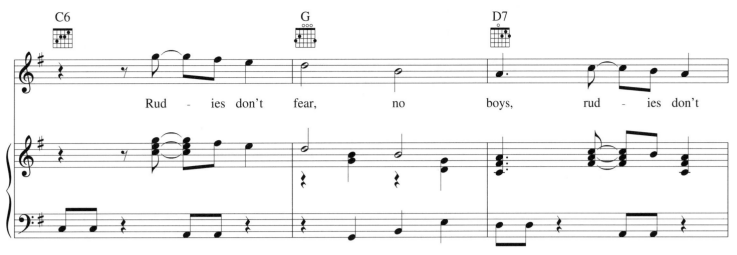

Rud - ies don't fear, no boys, rud - ies don't

fear. Rough - er than rough,

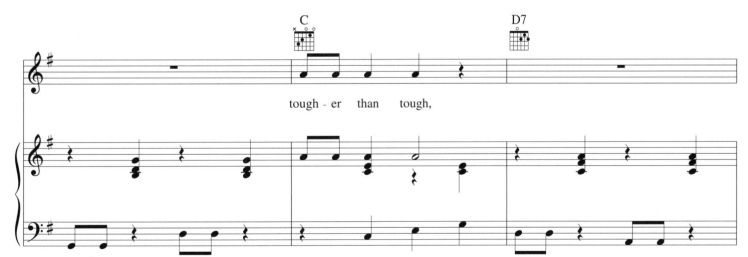

tough - er than tough,

strong like li - on, we are i - ron.

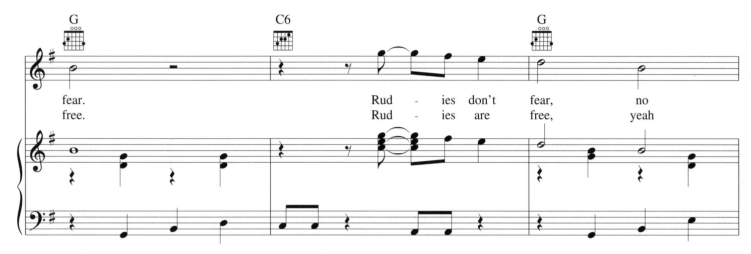

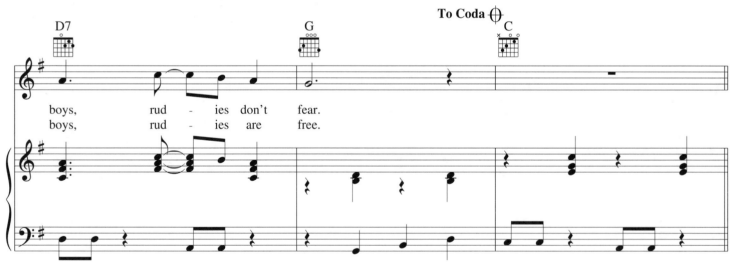

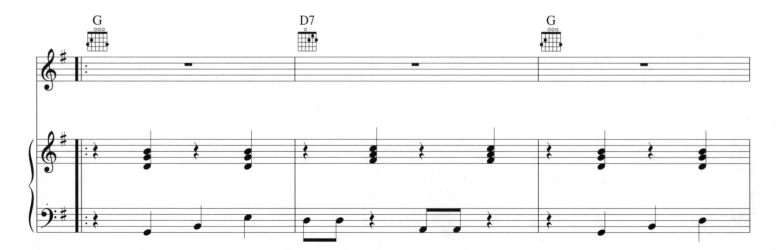

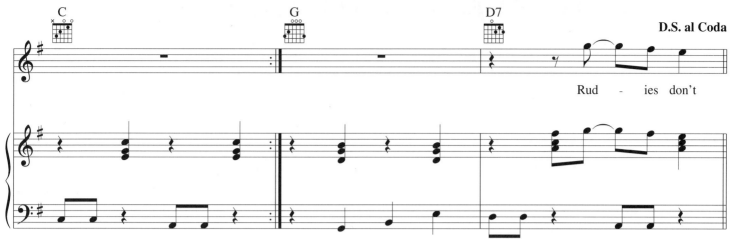

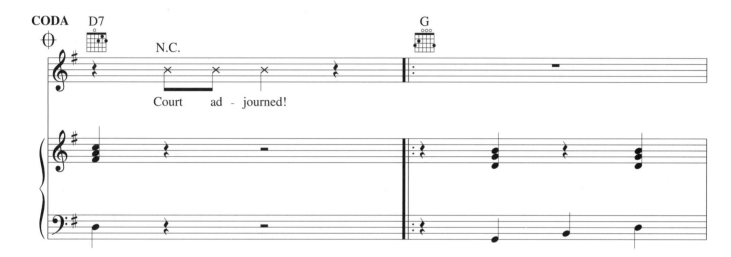

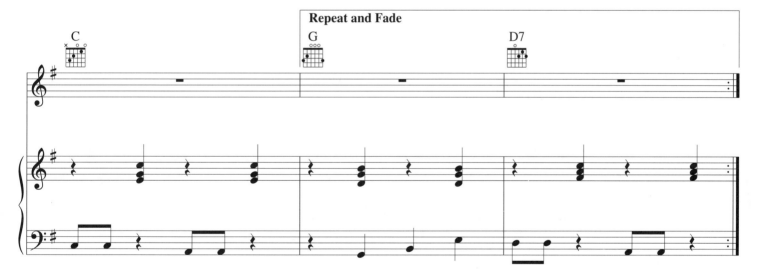

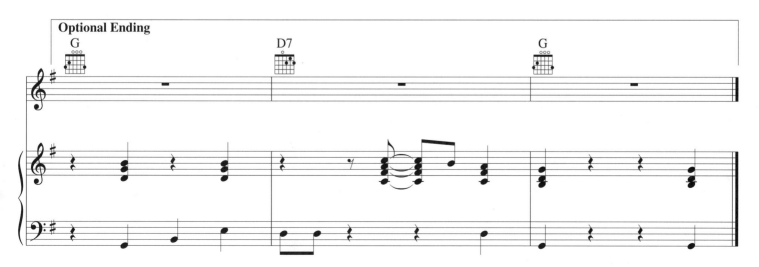

UPTOWN TOP RANKING

Words and Music by ERROL THOMPSON,
ALTHIA FORREST and DONNA REID

Moderate Reggae

See me in my heels and ting. Them chicks say we hip and

ting. You don't-a know an'-thing. We'll

have them go-in' and ting. Now part no

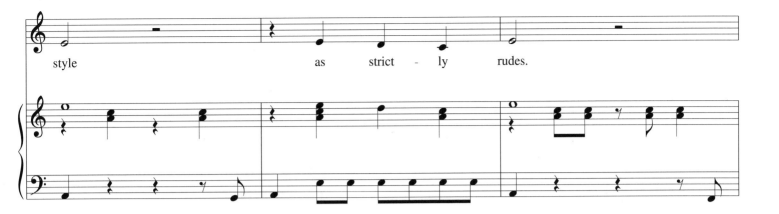

style as strict - ly rudes.

Now part no style as strict - ly

rudes. See me 'pon the road and you not call out to me. Do you

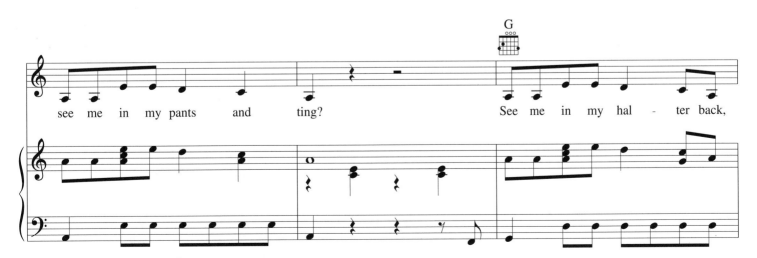

see me in my pants and ting? See me in my hal - ter back,

see me give you heart at - tack.

Am

Give me lit - tle beers not know why not no ways, up - town top rank -

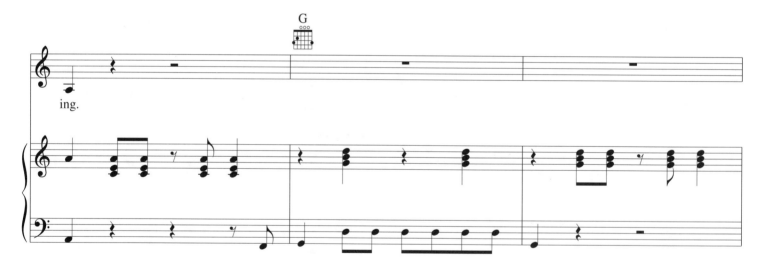

G

ing.

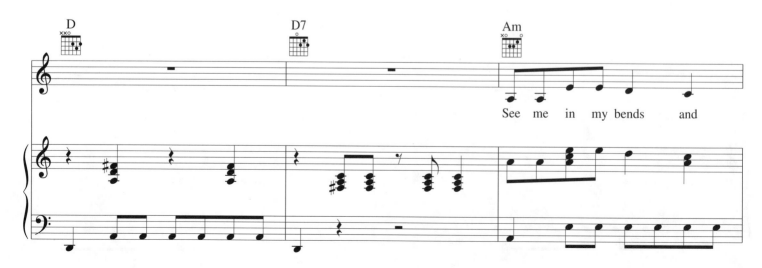

D   **D7**   **Am**

See me in my bends and

Should I

see me in a rank - ing dread? Chick, are we jam-ming an' -
Watch or we chuck it and ting. You know we cock - y suit and

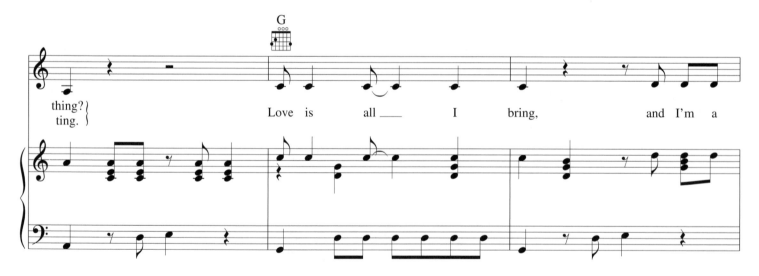

thing?} Love is all ___ I bring, and I'm a
ting.}

cock - y suit and ting. Now part no

lov - in' are you at is a by long for me. } Do you see me in my pants and
See me 'pon the road and you not call out to me. }

See me in my hal - ter back,

See me give you heart at - tack. Give me lit - tle beers not know

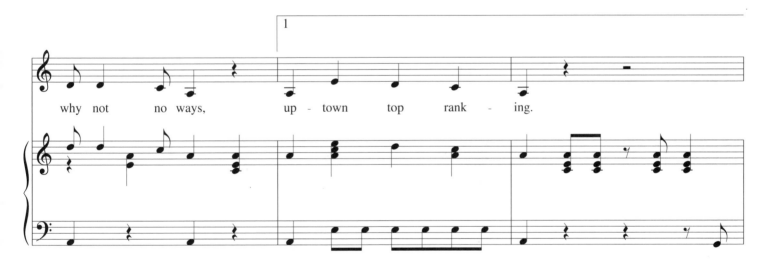

why not no ways, up - town top rank - ing.

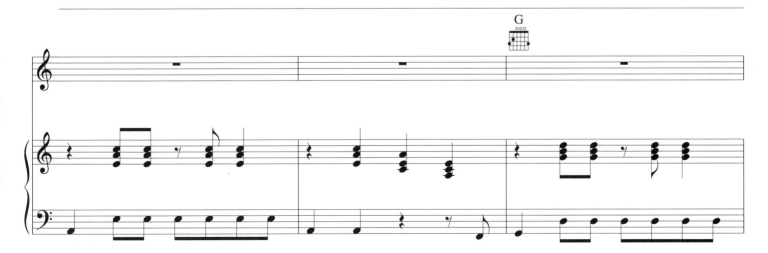

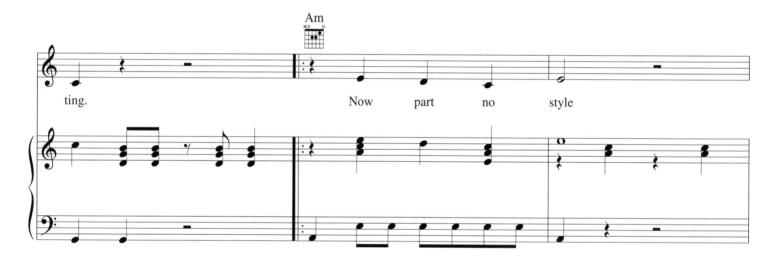

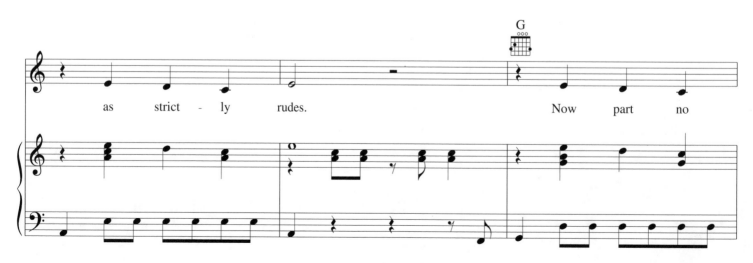

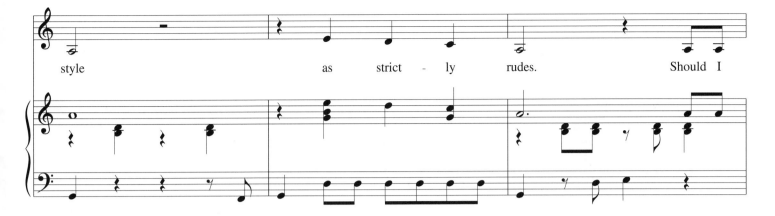

style   as strict - ly rudes.   Should I

Am

see me in a rank - ing dread?   Chick, are we jam - ming and

G

ting?   Love is all ___ I bring,   and I'm a

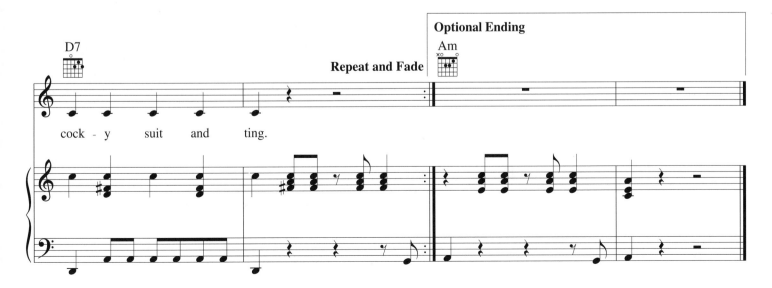

D7   **Repeat and Fade**   **Optional Ending**   **Am**

cock - y suit and ting.

WAR INA BABYLON

By LEE PERRY
and MAX ROMEO

Moderately

It's e - vil out there.

War in - a Bab - y - lon, tri - bal

war in a Bab - y - lon.   Look at that!   It's e - vil out there.

What you say?   It's e - vil out there.   Oh yeah.

War in - a Bab - y - lon,   tri - bal war in - a Bab - y - lon.

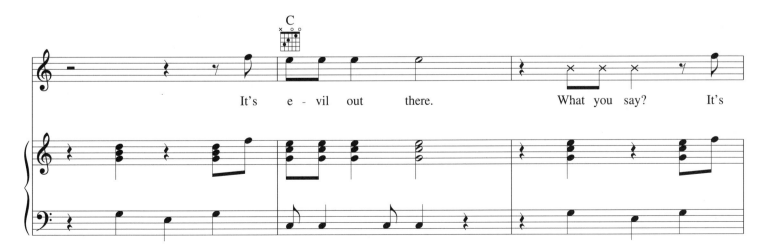

It's e - vil out there.   What you say?   It's

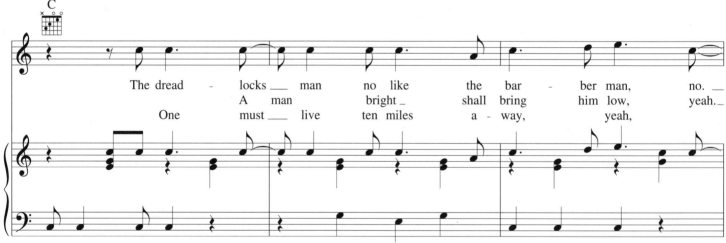

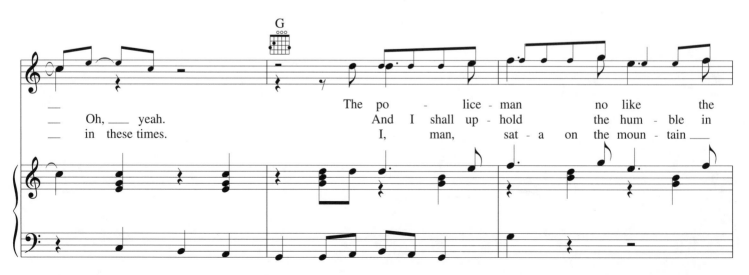

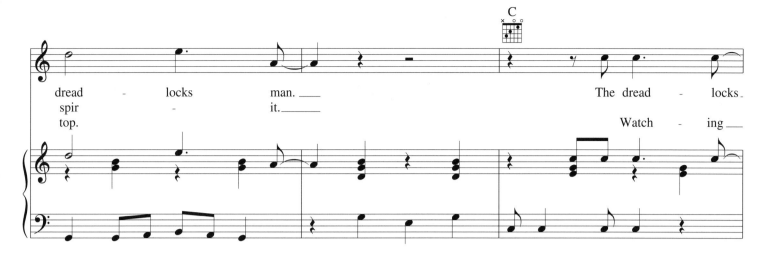

dread - locks man. ___ The dread - locks ___
spir - it. ___ Watch - ing ___
top.

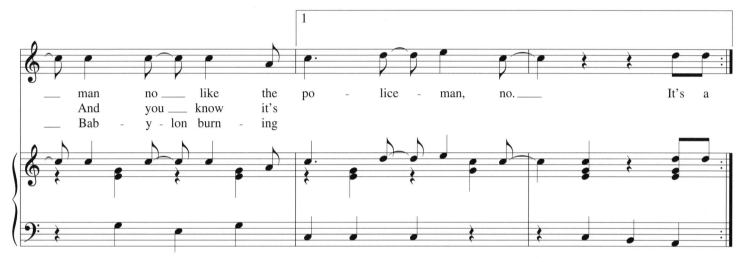

1

___ man no ___ like the po - lice - man, no. ___ It's a
And you ___ know it's
___ Bab - y - lon burn - ing

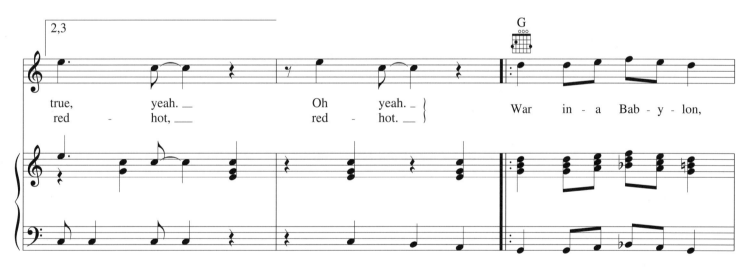

2,3

true, yeah. ___ Oh yeah. ___ } War in - a Bab - y - lon,
red - hot, ___ red - hot. ___ }

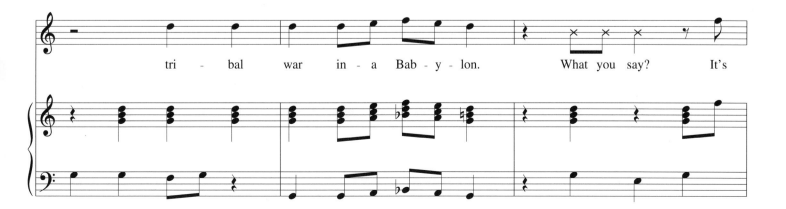

tri - bal war in - a Bab - y - lon. What you say? It's

4th time
To Coda

e - vil out there. So what you do if it's light out there?

Oh yeah. Oh yeah. Doo _____ doo _ doo _

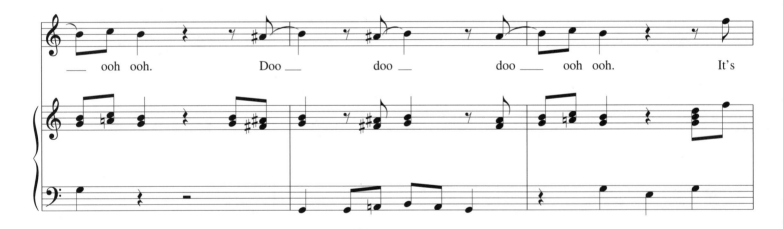

_ ooh ooh. Doo _ doo _ doo _ ooh ooh. It's

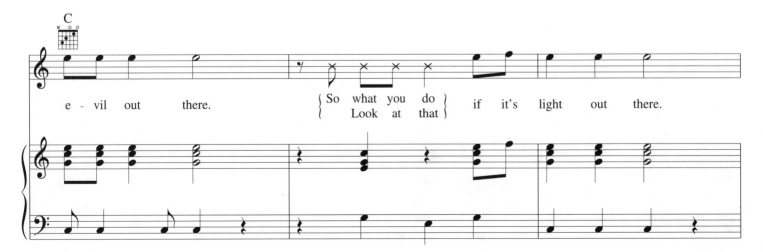

e - vil out there. { So what you do } if it's light out there.
{ Look at that }

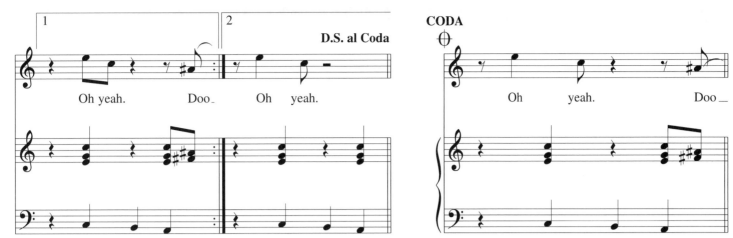

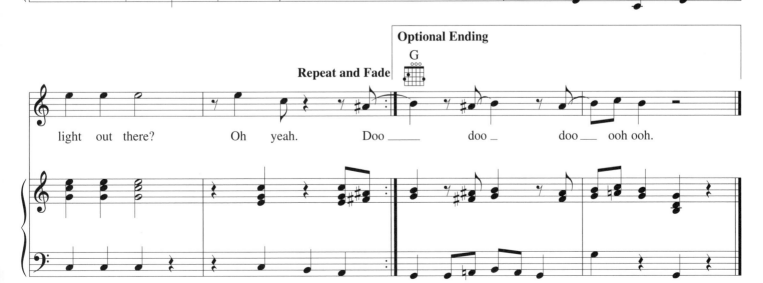

WICKED IN BED

Words and Music by CLEVELAND BROWNE,
WYCLIFFE JOHNSON and REXTON GORDON

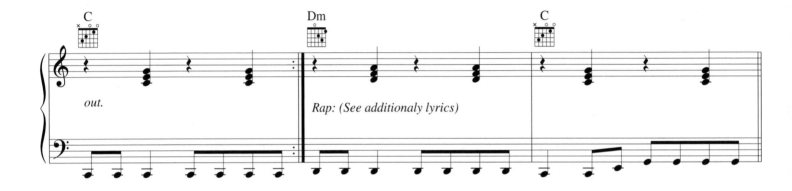

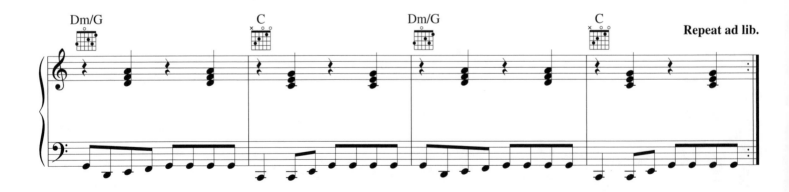

Intro: Dead woke! Whirl-a girl cry you out.
Dead woke! Step up! And now pilé.

Rap: There's a person: I am man, man. And-a wicked in the bed, a wicked man.
And man in the bed, I am man, man. And-a wicked in the bed, a wicked man. And man in the bed.
Now all the girls go tell the world if I am wicked in bed, a man, man. And-a wicked in the...
Now all the girls go tell the world if I am wicked in bed, a wicked man.
And man in the bed, I am man, man. And-a wicked in the bed, a wicked man. And man in the bed, ah.
Enough in me bed, me don't want a friend, ah. No one holding me.
No one hate me now, promote mi-mi-mind. Our ma-ma-moms are dead.
I'm proud to make a shanty, man. I'm on my-my gate, I am man, man.
And-a wicked in the bed, a wicked man. And man in the bed, I am man, man.
And-a wicked in the bed, a wicked man. And man in the bed, ah.
Enough in a bed. He play spot a Negro with doll-ear-a, and sexy lingo.
Go tell the world I have the girls spread your leg. I am man, man.
And-a wicked in the bed, a wicked man. And man in the bed, I am man, man.
And-a wicked in the bed, a wicked man. And man in the bed.
Now all the girls go tell the world if I am wicked in bed, a wicked man. And man in the bed, ah.
When they layin' down, in on my bed from tryin' to sleep, from me tour to me head.
And come from my right, come from the left dey come beggin'.
Give them the lovin' and then they'll stop beggin'. Give them the money, they may not look like much.
I am man, man. And-a wicked in the bed, a wicked man. And man in the bed, a man, man.
And-a wicked in the bed, a wicked man. And man in the bed, ah.
Enough in my bed, me don't want a friend, ah. No one holding me.
No one hate me now, promote mi-mi-mind. Our ma-ma-moms are dead.
I'm proud to make a shanty, now. I'm on my-my bed.
I am man, man. And-a wicked in the bed, a wicked man. And man in a..
Now all the girls go tell the world dat I'm-a wicked in bed, a wicked man. And man in a...
Now all the girls go tell the world dat I'm-a wicked in bed, a wicked man.
And man in the bed, I am man, man. And-a wicked in the bed, a wicked man. And, man in the bed, ah.
Dey all call me love. They come jump up on me bed, ah. Dey land my reef. Dey rode on my divan bed, ah.
No start jumpin' teacher jump on our head, ah. No one holding me.
No one hate me now, promote mi-mi-mind. Our ma-ma-moms are dead.
I'm proud to make a shanty now. I'm on my-my bed.
I am man, man. And-a wicked in the bed, a wicked man. And man in the bed, now
(Fade)

007 (SHANTY TOWN)

By DESMOND DEKKER

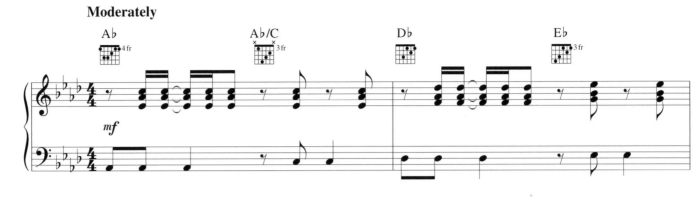

O - O - Sev - en, ___

O - O - Sev - en ___ at O - cean E -

lev - en, ___ and the rude boys at the wheel.

WELDING

Words and Music by
ROY REID

Spoken: I's called into the fields. Now sister, love, you got to wait until I

have my means, yah.   Yeah.

1. Weld - ing ___ now where the
2.-7. (See additional lyrics) Vocal ad lib.

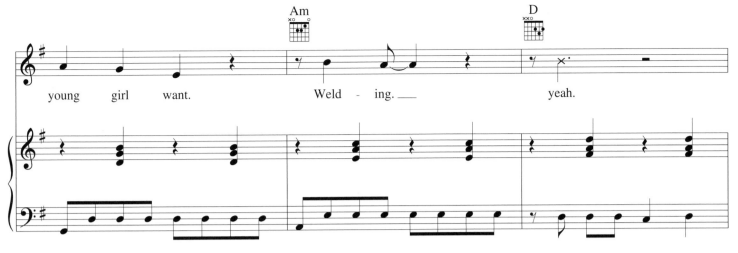

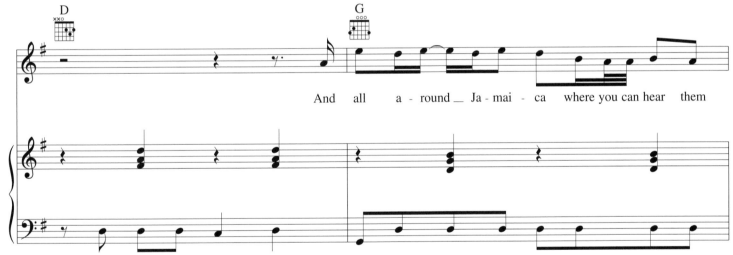

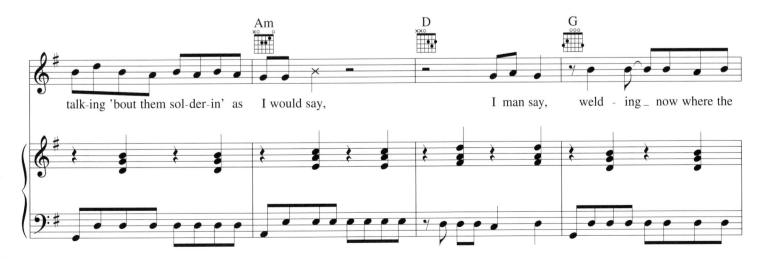

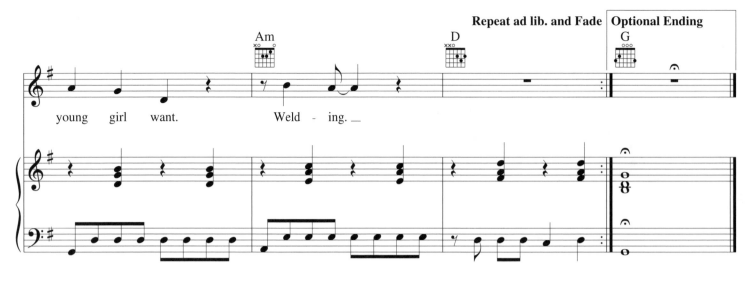

Additional Lyrics

And I kinda like my hot, silly torch. I can make them young girl move like a roach.
Yeah, and keep them soldering.
Solderin' a-where the whole lady want. Soldering, yeah.
Solderin' a-where the whole woman want. Soldering.

I man say welding now where the damsel want. Welding.
Higher the mountain, the greener the grass. Blacker the girl, the sweeter her...
Welding now where the young girl want. Welding.
Higher the monkey climb, the more we may expose. You can't think that you gotta stay on everything, there's no bed of rose.

Welding now where the rudes man want. Welding, yeah.
Deal with the damsel and deal with the heart. Welding, yeah.
Kill with the dart and even the whole lady too. Welding.
Weld them until they become-a black and blue. Welding.

Girly kind of walkin' up the street in a quick march while the train is sitting and the men all be welding torch. I say,
Welding-a where the damsel want. Yeah.
Gal climb tree and pick a monkey while a dread down steals a wholer pimp.
I say welding now where the... Welding.

Man in a house, a Mickey Mouse. While the girl outside-a get her sauce. I say,
Welding now where the damsel them want now. Welding all over town, yah.

Way down to Midway coming through from Mambo Bay way, way over to boat and down the Ocho Rios you can hear me say,
Welding now where the damsel them want now. Welding.

Scouty high, and scouty low, in counties stand up to the stare where b-blow I say.
Welding is where the sister they want now. Welding, yeah.
Welding now where the dread them love, yah. Welding. Move!
Welding where *(Fade)*...

* *Vocal is sung ad lib. using melodic phrases indicated in written melody. Each line represents a four measure phrase.*